SOUNION

THE TEMPLE OF POSEIDON

Publishers: George A. Christopoulos, John C. Bastias
Translation: David Hardy
Managing Editor: Efi Karpodini
Art Director: Angela Simou
Special Photography: Spyros Tsavdaroglou, Yannis Scouroyannis
Colour separation: Pietro Carlotti

SOUNION

THE TEMPLE OF POSEIDON

A.B. TATAKI

Archaeologist

EKDOTIKE ATHENON S.A.
Athens 1992

ISBN 960-213-136-5

Copyright © 1978, 1979, 1983, 1984
by
Ekdotike Athenon S.A.
1, Vissarionos St., Athens 106 72
Printed in Greece

CONTENTS

1. *Cape Sounion, with the temple of Poseidon from the west.*

2. *The temple of Poseidon at Sounion in the sunset.*

3. *Part of the south colonnade of the temple of Poseidon in the sunset.*

4-5. Cape Sounion, with the temple of Poseidon in the sunset.

INTRODUCTION

The promontory of Sounion is the southernmost tip of Attica. Here, on a windswept bluff rising above the Aegean sea, stands the temple of Poseidon, one of the most impressive classical monuments to have survived to the present day. It was built shortly after the middle of the 5th century B.C., during the same period that saw the beginning of work on the great monuments on the Athenian acropolis.

Archaeology has proved conclusively that this was not the first temple to occupy this uniquely beautiful site; nor was it the only one in the area, for the buildings belonging to the sanctuary of the goddess Athena are quite close by. Even though it is today in ruins, however, it still dominates the surrounding countryside from its site on the highest point of the region, and it is easy to see that in its heyday it must also have set the seal of its character on the whole area.

In ancient times large numbers of worshippers used to make the journey to these two neighbouring sanctuaries, most of them coming from different parts of Attica, and a few from further afield; on their arrival they will have been suffering from fatigue to a greater or lesser degree, depending on the distance they had travelled, the availability or otherwise of transport, and the intensity of the Attic sun during the journey. Nowadays, Sounion receives countless visitors from every part of the world. The motives that bring them here have changed, of course, as have the conditions under which they make the journey. There are now two roads linking Sounion with Athens, which means that the trip can be made swiftly and in comfort, and that it is possible to take a different route on

6. Cape Sounion, with the temple of Poseidon on its flat summit.

7-9. *Aerial view of Cape Sounion with the ruins of the sanctuary of Poseidon.*

the return journey and thus see two entirely different facets of the Attic countryside. The coast road (67 kms) runs along the south-west coast, and the old road (64 kms), through the large villages in the Mesogeia, affords a view of inland Attica.

The traveller heading east by boat from Piraeus invariably awaits with anticipation the sight of the columns of the temple of Poseidon, perhaps gleaming white in the sun, perhaps appearing through the mist in the distance, depending on the time of day and the weather. It is a sight whose beauty never ceases to impress.

The promontory, whish lies 31 nautical miles SE of Piraeus, has been dubbed *Kavokolones* (cape of columns) by sailors, after the columns rising on its summit. The first travellers of modern times to visit Sounion, who have left us those beautiful drawings of the antiquities of the area as they were before archaeological excavation began, also knew it and referred to it by this name. These travellers also preserved a number of legends connected with the ruined temple in comparatively recent times to account for the damage it has suffered at different periods — damage that not only derived from natural causes but that was for the most part the work of man. Popular imagination conceived of the temple as the palace of a "princess," or of a governor or, better still, of Alexander the Great himself; this naturally tempted some to investigate the building, and to wreak enormous destruction in a fruitless search for hidden treasure. Despite all it has suffered, however, the monument still preserves today the incredible vigour and splendour that classical buildings alone never lose.

The historical background

It is impossible to view Sounion and its history in isolation from Attica, of which it is an integral part. Sounion was one of the demes of ancient Attica, belonging originally to the tribe of Leontis, though it became part of the tribe of Attalis after 200 B.C. Of the two sanctuaries in the area, one, that of Athena, was of mainly local importance; that of Poseidon, however, was closely connected with the might of Athens, for in addition to its role as a religious centre, it was also one of the most important forts in Attica.

The region was inhabited at an early point in time: so much is clear from the existence of prehistoric tombs, the earliest of them dating from the 3rd millenium B.C. The earliest written source to refer to Sounion is the *Odyssey,* in which Homer describes it as a sanctuary *(Odys.* III, 278: *"but when we came to the sanctuary of Sounion...");* in the 8th century B.C. at least, then, the place appears to have been a centre of worship. Homer further relates in the *Odyssey* how Phrontis, Menelaos' helmsman, died at Sounion during the journey home from Troy, and was buried there.

10. The small bays and inlets on the east coast of Cape Sounion.

The two sanctuaries seem to have developed alongside each other during the following century, a period that saw the expansion of many other Greek sanctuaries. Attica took no part in the colonisation movement that played such an important role in the life of other developed areas of Greece at this time (8th-7th centuries B.C.). It still had a rural economy, and the sanctuary buildings were made of wood and other impermanent materials, while the statues of the gods were simple wooden *xoana*.

During the last part of the 7th century B.C., in the years following the legislation of Dracon, there was a very important development in Attic art — a bold innovation characterised mainly by a move towards the monumental. The figure of the *kouros,* the powerful youth, made its first appearance and quickly became a dominant form. *Kouroi* were erected as dedications in sanctuaries or on the sumptuous tombs of wealthy young men.

About 600 B.C. a number of *kouroi* of larger than life size were set up in the precinct of Poseidon, and also in the sanctuary of Athena. These youths, contemporaries of Solon, look straight ahead with a freshness and eagerness that mark the beginning of a new period in Attic art. It is also the beginning of a new phase in the history of the sanctuaries at Sounion, especially that of Poseidon. The history of Attica took a new direction after the reforms of the wise law-giver Solon, who was also a lyric poet and one of the seven sages of ancient Greece.

At about the same time as the *kouroi* were standing at Sounion (National Archaeological Museum), a great change took place on the Athenian acropolis: the temple of Athena was embellished by the addition of sculptures carved in porous limestone. The first temple of Poseidon at Sounion was also of porous stone, as were most archaic buildings; we do not know, however, the exact date of its construction. During the 6th century the wealth of Athens increased, and major public works were carried out in the city under the tyrant Peisistratos (561-527 B.C.). One of the sources of Athenian wealth was located very close to Sounion: this was the silver mines nearby at Laurion, which were worked by slaves. There was a large slave market at Sounion, to cater for the demands of the contractors of the mines. On obtaining their freedom, many of the slaves stayed on in the deme as *Sounieis politai* (citizens of Sounion). There are a considerable number of remains of the mineworkings in the region of Laurion. The Attic silver coins known as *Laurian Owls* were famous in antiquity.

The Persian Wars in the first part of the 5th century B.C. put the whole of the Greek world in a state of turmoil. The rich vein of silver discovered at Laurion at this time was precisely what Athens needed. The enormous potential that lay within the grasp of the city as a result of this unexpected stroke of fortune depended on its proper exploitation, and this was ensured by the statesman Themistocles, who proposed to his fellow-citizens that the profits from the mines should be used to finance the construction of a war fleet. His proposal was accepted (483 B.C.), and its implementation had enormous significance for the future history of Athens. The Persians were defeated and fled, leaving behind them a series of ruined sanctuaries, amongst which were the Athenian acropolis and the two sanctuaries at Sounion (480 B.C.). Herodotos relates (VIII, 121) that after their victory over the Persians, the Greeks sent one of the captured Phoenician ships to Sounion, where it was dedicated in the

11. The temple of Poseidon and the fortress on Cape Sounion from the north.

12. The east coast at Sounion.

sanctuary of Poseidon, in honour of the god who had secured their victory at sea.

The end of the Persian Wars marked the beginning of a great period in the history of Athens. One of the major factors contributing to the advancement of the city at this time was the foundation in 478 B.C. of the Delian Confederacy, a league of coastal and island cities presided over by Athens herself. A large proportion of Aegean trade passed into Athenian hands, the city became an important industrial centre, and its population increased considerably. After a few years, the Persian threat ceased to exist and with it the original purpose of the Confederacy, the nature and aims of which changed. Athens became an imperial power, wielding authority over a large empire, and her former allies became subject states. These changes are connected with the emergence and domination of Pericles in the political life of Athens, and extended over a much wider area than the question of her relations with the allies, to affect every sphere of the life of the city.

It is no coincidence that this period, during which so many brilliant intellects were active in Athens, is known to history by the name of Pericles: the years of his political activity (461-429 B.C.) coincide with the greatest days Athens has ever known. A large number of exceptionally gifted men lived in the city at this time, and it became the intellectual capital of the whole of Greece; their number included many Greeks from outside Attica, especially Ionia.

In 454 B.C., the treasury of the Confederacy was moved to Athens from Delos, where it had originally been located, and a few years later, in 448 B.C., the decision was taken to expend a large proportion of allied funds on beautifying the city and the acropolis.

The later temple of Poseidon at Sounion was built between 444 and 440 B.C., and most probably formed part of Pericles' building programme. This programme, and the expenditure of enormous sums of money on "luxury" buildings that it entailed, naturally furnished easy arguments for Pericles' political opponents. He himself believed that the programme, carried out under his supervision, was for the good of the city, to which he was totally dedicated, and he deployed his amazing oratorical powers, on which all the sources are agreed, to destroy the arguments of the opposition. When accused of wasting vast sums of money, he retorted that he would charge it to his own account, not to theirs (by which he meant the public) but that he would have his own name inscribed on the buildings as dedicator.

By these means he not only ensured the continuation of the building programme, but also rid himself of his main political opponent: Thucydides son of Melesias was ostracised, involving exile for 10 years, in 444/3 B.C., the year in which the foundations for the temple of Poseidon were laid. Thenceforth Pericles' position was stronger than ever. He was elected general with sweeping powers each year until his death, and this enabled him to implement in all their detail the plans he had for the city.

While the temple of Poseidon was being built at Sounion, Herodotos of Halicarnassos, the father of history, spent a number of years in Athens, a city of which he was a great admirer. It appears to have been his admiration for and association with Pericles that inspired him to convert his work into a history of the Persian Wars. During this same period (444/3 B.C.) Athens played a leading role in the founding of Thourioi, a panhellenic colony in southern Italy, near the site of the city of Sybaris, which was in ruins by that date.

The next time that Sounion emerges into the light of history was during the course of the Peloponnesian War (431-404 B.C.), at a point when Athenian affairs were taking a turn for the worse. This war broke out a mere 15 years after the conclusion of a 30 years peace between Athens and Sparta (446/5 B.C.), and ultimately resulted in disaster for both protagonists. The population of Attica, which is calculated to have numbered 172,000 Athenian citizens, 28,000 resident aliens and 115,000 slaves at this date, suffered particularly badly from the annual invasions by the Spartan army.

Thucydides, the historian of the war, informs us that when the Spartans under Agis seized Dekeleia and severed Athenian communications with Boeotia by way of Oropos, the Athenians responded by deciding to strengthen the fort on the tip of the promontory at Sounion — in the area, that is, of the sanctuary of Poseidon (Thucydides VII-VIII). By so doing, Athens secured the safe passage of ships off the headland and thereby ensured the transport of vital supplies from Euboea, mainly of corn to feed the population (412 B.C.).

The Athenians had been quick to grasp the strategic and economic significance of the site at Sounion and strengthened the fortress. The inscriptions discovered during the course of the excavations indicate that they also established a military force there under the command of a general, whose duties included preserving the defence walls in a good state of repair. Ships put in at Sounion whenever the weather conditions prevented them from sailing to the east or north Aegean, and it appears to have been at Sounion that the *theoric* ship lay at anchor, thereby delaying the execution of Socrates, as Plato relates in his *Crito*. Finally, it was here that the Aeginetans captured the Athenian sacred ship as it was transporting the *theoroi* (sacred ambassadors) to Delos, shortly before the Persian Wars (Herodotos VI, 87).

The fort at Sounion was regarded by the Athenians as one of the most important in Attica. It was also closely linked with the history of Athens during the period when, despite the loss of her former political power, the city was still trying to escape the control of Macedonia. One such attempt was the Chremonidean War (267-261 B.C.); this proved a failure not only for Athens itself, which was subjected to a protracted siege, but also for her allies in the war, Sparta and Egypt. While Athens was under siege by the forces of Antigonos Gonatas, the Spartan forces were routed at the Isthmos and never reached their destination. The Egyptian fleet sent to the assistance of the Athenians by Ptolemy Philadelphos was unable to affect a landing near Piraeus or at Phaleron, for these areas were covered by the Macedonian fleet.

Matters became extremely difficult for the Athenians when Antigonos captured the fort at Sounion and thus made himself master of the Attic countryside. The island to the west of Sounion, known as the island of Patroclos, or Gaïdouronisi, was used by the Egyptian fleet as a base in its operations against Antigonos. Patroclos, the admiral of that fleet, set up a camp on the uninhabited island close to Attica, and part of the improvised wall built on this occasion still survives.

Athens was ultimately captured by the Macedonians and lost its political independence until 229 B.C. In this year Aratos, the leader of the

13. Part of the peribolos for the defence of the headland, with the west coast of Cape Sounion in the background.

Achaean League, having failed to arouse the Athenians to revolt, turned to other means that immediately had the desired effect of clearing the Macedonian garrisons out of Attica: he bribed Diogenes, the garrison commander, who surrendered all the forts in Attica to the Athenians.

Sounion and the sanctuaries there appear to have entered a period of sharp decline in the lst century B.C. An indication of this decline and the abandonment of the sanctuaries is that during the rule of Augustus (31

B.C. - A.D. 14) the temple of Athena was taken to Athens and erected in the Agora, where a few pieces of it have been found.

In the 2nd century A.D., Pausanias toured various parts of the Greek world and recorded his impressions and the information he had collected about the history of each site and the form of its monuments in earlier times. His chapter on Attica opens with a description of Sounion, which he appears to have seen only from the boat as he sailed to Piraeus. On the crest of the promontory he saw a temple which he assumed to be that of Athena, and the information he collected concerning Attica similarly includes the assertion that there was a temple of this goddess at Sounion. It is clear that Pausanias' information about this area was inaccurate and that he was unaware of the fate of the temple of Athena (though it had been removed to Athens only a few years before his time); as a result he gave rise to the misconception, which has persisted into modern times, that the temple of Poseidon was in fact a temple to Athena. He was probably so preoccupied with his desire to visit the city of Pallas that he did not always exercise proper care in recording details connected with the sanctuaries of other gods. During the course of his description of the monuments on the Athenian acropolis, he mentions the statue of Athena Promachos that stood there, and is at pains to note that the tip of Athena's spear could be seen by anyone travelling by ship from the direction of Sounion. We may perhaps assume that in his eagerness to see the gleaming spear of Pheidias' bronze masterpiece, he forgot about the temple of Poseidon, which must still have been known, even though it had been abandoned.

Elsewhere in his chapter on Attica Pausanias mentions Makronisos, an island to the east of the promontory of Sounion, which he calls the "island of Helen." According to one version of the legend Helen, Menelaos' wife, disembarked here on the return journey from Troy. In the middle of the 2nd century B.C., the fort at Sounion was captured by 1000 rebellious slaves, from the mines at Laurion. Little is known of Sounion in the following periods.

In more recent times both Sounion and Makronisos were used as pirate strongholds, particularly in the 14th century A.D. The 17th century travellers who had the stamina and determination to visit this isolated spot found the temple in ruins. It appears from their accounts that 9 columns on the south side and 5 on the north were all that was standing of the temple of Poseidon at that time.

The romantic poet Lord Byron, one of the most famous of the philhellenes, visited the ruined temple at the beginning of the 19th century. Byron lived a good many years of his life in Greece, which at that period was aspiring to freedom and independence, and died in 1824 during the siege of Mesolongi. He fell under the inspiring spell of Sou-

14. Part of the wall of the fortress, originally thought to be a granary.

nion, the "Marbled Steep" as he described it *(Don Juan)*, of the view towards the islands of the Aegean *(Giaour)*, and of the sanctuary of "Tritonia" on "Colonna's cliff" *(Childe Harold's Pilgrimage)*.

> *Save where some solitary column mourns*
> *Above its prostrate brethren of the cave;*
> *Save where Tritonia's airy shrine adorns*
> *Colonna's cliff, and gleams along the wave;*
> *Save o'er some warrior's half-forgotten grave,*
> *Where the grey stones and unmolested grass*
> *Ages, but not oblivion, feebly brave,*
> *While strangers only not regardless pass,*
> *Lingering like me, perchance, to gaze and sigh "Alas!"*

> *(Childe Harold's Pilgrimage, Canto II, 86).*

Tritonia is an epithet of Athena, to whom he thought the temple was dedicated. Sounion became part of Byron's poetry just as his own name, carved on a column, became part of the temple; it is now one of the main attractions. Visitors have been in the habit of carving their names on the ancient marble from a very early point in time. The custom began as early as the first centuries A.D., and may be observed on numerous ancient monuments; the temple at Sounion, however, surpasses all of them in terms of the numbers of the names carved on it. Those who are arrogant enough to carve their names in this way are guilty of an act of defilement that can rarely be justified — perhaps only in cases like that of the charming Lord Byron.

THE MYTHOLOGICAL TRADITION

Poseidon and Athena

The worship of Athena was widespread in ancient Greece, and was to be found in many areas outside Attica, though the goddess had a special relationship with this region. There was a whole series of sanctuaries of Athena within the Greek world proper: on the Athenian acropolis, at Delphi, at Lindos and the other cities on Rhodes, at Tegea, and elsewhere. This is also true of the colonies in the west, where temples to Athena have survived, or are attested, at Akragas, Syracuse, Poseidonia (Paestum) and Selinous, and of the Greek cities of Asia Minor: Priene, Pergamon and others.

The worship of Poseidon was also very widely disseminated

15. Depiction of Poseidon by the Amasis painter on an Attic amphora of the 6th century B.C. The god has long tresses and beard; he holds a trident in his hand and wears a chiton and a himation. (Paris, Cabinet des Médailles)

throughout the Greek world and among the Greeks at the colonies. In addition to the temples at Sounion and the Corinthian Isthmus, there were sanctuaries to the god in many parts of Greece, such as Kalauria (Poros), Thasos, Delos and Tainaron. There was probably also a temple to Poseidon at Akragas, and the god had his own *temenos,* or sacred precinct, at Delphi. Euripides, in his satyr-play, the *Cyclops,* alludes to the different places at which Poseidon was worshipped, Sounion being amongst them. Every four years, boat races were held in honour of the god (Lysias, *Defense against a charge of taking bribes*).

The two deities clashed with each other for sovereignty over Attica, yet at Sounion their sanctuaries were separated by a bare 500 metres. A few years after the construction of the temple of Poseidon, the confrontation between the two was chosen as the theme for the west pediment of the Parthenon, the most important temple ever dedicated to Athena.

Poseidon, son of Cronos and Rhea and brother of Zeus, was considered to be one of the ancient Greek gods. He was originally worshipped as god of springs and rivers, and eventually established himself as god of the sea, to whom all the pre-hellenic gods and spirits of the sea owed allegiance. He was one of the twelve great gods of the Olympic pantheon, though not quite as strong as Zeus. His palace, where he lived with his wife Amphitrite, was in the depths of the sea. When Poseidon conceived the desire to become lord of Attica he stuck his trident into the rock of the Athenian acropolis, and caused sea water to issue from it.

Athena, the daughter born from the head of Zeus, and the goddess who had taught men the arts by which they had grown great, chose other means to establish her sway over the region that was fated to become hers: she planted the first olive tree next to the place where Poseidon had struck the rock with his trident. The god wanted to settle the dispute by means of a duel, but Zeus intervened to prevent this. The question was eventually resolved by the council of the gods, which decreed that the goddess had the greater claim to Attica since she had bestowed the greater gift upon it.

At Sounion the two deities were peaceful neighbours, Poseidon, of course, having the better site and the more important of the two sanctuaries. The Athenians did not neglect the god, but built him a splendid temple consonant with his standing in the Olympic pantheon. In this fashion they repaid the honour he had done them in wishing to become their protector, and also secured his protection for all those who sailed round the usually stormy promontory of Sounion. Every four years, in the 5th century at least, they held a festival at Sounion, and the Athenian officials travelled with great pomp in a special ship to take part in the ceremonies.

16. Vase painting of Athena of the 5th century B.C. The goddess wears the aegis on her breast, and holds a spear in one hand and her helmet in the other. (Musei Vaticani)

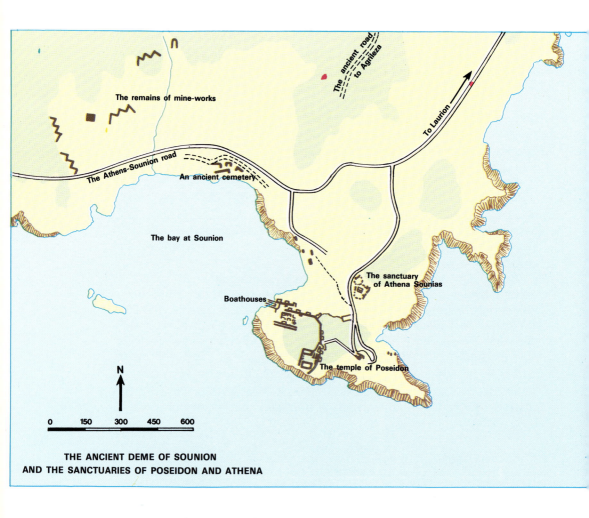

The remains of mine-works

The ancient road to Agrileza

To Laurion

The Athens-Sounion road

An ancient cemetery

The bay at Sounion

The sanctuary of Athena Sounias

Boathouses

The temple of Poseidon

N

0   150   300   450   600

**THE ANCIENT DEME OF SOUNION
AND THE SANCTUARIES OF POSEIDON AND ATHENA**

EXCAVATIONS

The earliest archaeological investigation of the temple of Poseidon, which was on a limited scale, was undertaken by members of the Society of Dilletanti at the end of the 18th century. Shortly afterwards, in 1825, the area around the temple was investigated by a French mission led by Blouet, who followed the example of the previous team and published plans and a commentary. The first excavation proper in the temple, however, was that by the German W. Dörpfeld in 1884. The Greek Archaeological Society began a series of excavations in 1897 that lasted until 1915, under the direction of V. Staï assisted by A. Orlandos. These excavations established the true identity of the temple, and also uncovered the sanctuary of Athena, some 500 metres from the sanctuary already known.

The sanctuary of Poseidon

The sanctuary of Poseidon occupied only one part of the fortified area of the promontory of Sounion. The modern entrance to this area does not correspond with the ancient, which was on the NW side of the enceinte, a long way from the entrance to the archaeological site. The visitor now enters through an opening in the wall between two of the towers that used to protect the eastern side. He then advances a short distance before turning left and proceeding to the highest point of the promontory and the site of the sanctuary.

This area was also the acropolis of the fortress. It was artificially levelled and has its own *peribolos,* or perimeter wall, which serves as a retaining wall for the terrace of the sanctuary; this was probably built at the end of the archaic period. Part of this *peribolos,* on the east side, is also part of the defensive enceinte of the fortress. The south side, most of which has been lost, was a continuation of the east, which curved around, thus giving the sanctuary the shape of a horse-shoe. The other two sides, the north and west, formed the boundary between the sanctuary and the fortress. They were very carefully built, in the isodomic style, of blocks of porous stone faced with marble; the east wall was polygonal. The dimensions of the area enclosed by the *peribolos* are 60 m. × 80 m.

The only entrance into the sanctuary was in the north side of the *peribolos* by means of what was, for the period, a magnificent *propylon.* Very little of this *propylon,* or of the neighbouring buildings, can be seen today, though a great deal can be deduced about the form of them. Both the exterior and interior façades of the *propylon* had two Doric columns *in antis* supporting the roof, which was in the form of a pediment. The building thus had the shape of a temple. Inside it there were two blocks, aligned with the columns so that, together with the side walls, they formed three separate entrances. The central, widest (2.20 m.) entrance was used mainly by wheeled traffic and animals for the sacrifices, while the other two were for pedestrians.

The plan of the building had many points of similarity with the *propylaia* on the Athenian acropolis, and use was made in it of two materials commonly found in the buildings of the period: marble and porous stone. According to one view, this combination, which there was no attempt to disguise, was employed for reasons of economy and belongs to a single chronological phase; other scholars, however, believe that the building was originally constructed of porous stone, and was later faced with marble in order to match the splendour of the temple.

To the right of the *propylaia* as one enters the sanctuary, and contiguous with them, there was a building whose entrance opened onto the area enclosed by the *peribolos,* and which was probably a guard-house. To the right of it again, was a *stoa* (portico) which ran along the rest of the north side of the sacred precinct. It was built of porous stone and was the largest of the *stoas* in the sanctuary, measuring 25 m. × 9 m. The *peribolos* was used as the rear wall of it, and the façade had 8 or 9 Doric columns. There was a second row of 6 fluted columns down the middle of it which, in the opinion of the excavator V. Staïs, came from the earlier temple of Poseidon, destroyed by the Persians.

The *stoa* appears to have been built after the *propylon,* and will have protected visitors to the sanctuary from the sun, the rain, and above all the strong wind that so often buffets this spot. This area served as a resting place for visitors, and it was later enlarged by the addition of a second *stoa,* 20.80 m. long, running along the west side of the precinct at right angles to the first. We do not know how many columns there were in the façade of this *stoa* but we do know that it was half as wide as the other and had no interior row of columns.

The fortification wall, the *propylon* and the *stoas* formed a frame for the temple, which stood on the highest point of the precinct, and indeed of the region. The stylobate of the temple is 6.42 m. higher than the

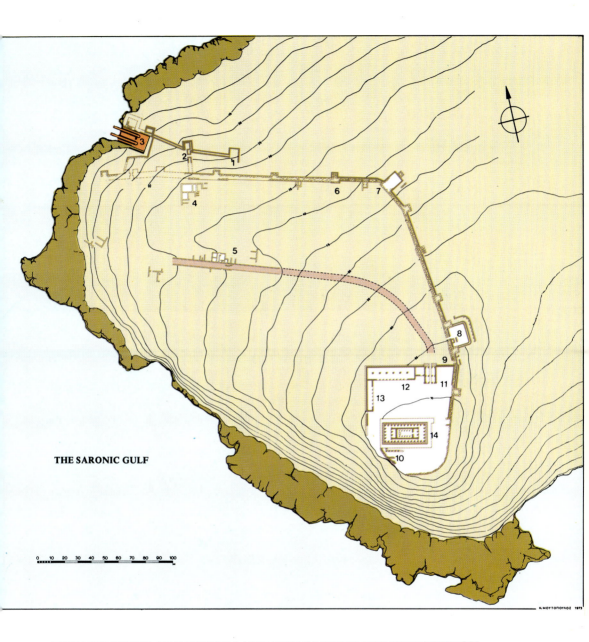

THE SARONIC GULF

0 10 20 30 40 50 60 70 80 90 100

Η. ΜΟΥΤΟΠΟΥΛΟΣ 1973

THE FORTRESS AT SOUNION AND THE SANCTUARY OF POSEIDON

1. *Probable location of the entrance to the fortified enclosure.*
2. *Tower.*
3. *Boathouses.*
4,5. *Remains of buildings.*
6,7. *Towers.*

8. *Rectangular area.*
9. *Small gate.*
10. *Remains of the early temple.*
11. *The propylon of the sanctuary.*
12,13. *Stoa.*
14. *Temple of Poseidon.*

propylon. We have already noted that the temple of Poseidon, built between 444 and 440 B.C., was not the first to be constructed on this site. A large temple of porous stone was built on precisely the same site during the archaic period; this temple was also Doric and had many points of similarity with the marble temple whose remains can still be seen today. The precise date of the first temple is not known, but it was probably built only a few years before its destruction at the hands of the Persians in 480 B.C. It is clear from the fluted columns later used in the large *stoa* on the north side of the sanctuary that the temple was not finished at the time it was destroyed. Material from it was also used later in the sanctuary of Athena.

The archaic temple was slightly smaller than that of the classical period; the dimensions of the stylobate were 30.20 m. × 13.06 m. compared with the 31.12 m. × 13.47 m. of the classical building. Both temples had the same number of columns — 6 on the short sides and 13 on the long (the columns at the corners counting twice). Parts of the archaic porous foundation can be seen at many points. The earlier temple appears to have had two rows of 5 columns along the inside of the walls of the *cella,* a feature that was not repeated in the later monument. Its dimensions and proportions show that the lost archaic temple was a very advanced building for its period, which accounts for the retention of the basic features of it in its successor about 50 years later.

The material used in the later temple was white marble from Agrileza, a quarry 4 kms to the north of the promontory, that supplied most of the marble for the buildings in the surrounding area. This marble does not contain iron, and therefore does not lose its colour with the passage of time but stays brilliant white, unlike Pentelic marble, which turns to warm tones of beige, pink or gold. It is soft, however, and wears easily. It appears to have been this property of the marble that decided the architect on an innovation in the fluting of the columns, which were only 16 in number, instead of the usual 20. The fact that the flutings were fewer meant that they were also shallower; the ridges between them were consequently not as sharp and therefore in less danger of wearing away on this very exposed site. One consequence of the reduction in the number of flutings will have been that the columns will have had a less imposing appearance. They had very slender proportions, and there was no *entasis* (the slight curve along the vertical axis that was a feature of the columns of this period), and these two features give them an almost Ionic appearance.

This was not the only innovation in the plan of the temple, however. It has a whole series of special features that make it a completely original building. The name of the 5th century architect responsible for it has been lost, though his work has survived. A comparative study of the buildings of this period has led scholars to the belief that this same architect was responsible for the plans of four known temples. These all have certain features in common, amounting to the personal trademark

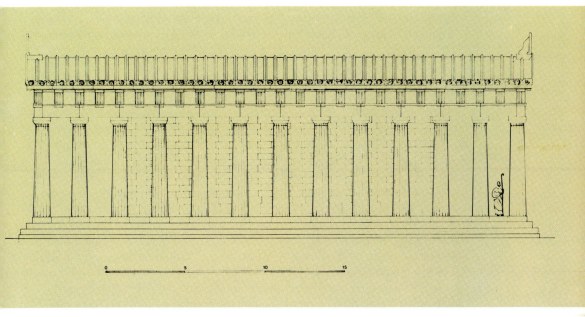

19. Reconstruction of the long side of the temple of Poseidon.

of a common creator, though at the same time they exhibit certain differences illustrative of the development of his work. The oldest of them is thought to be the temple of Hephaistos and Athena on the west side of the Athenian Agora, better known as the "Theseion." This temple is the best preserved ancient building in Greece, and the construction of it commenced in 449 B.C., two years before the beginning of work on the Parthenon. The temple of Poseidon was the second in the series of buildings by this same architect, and the completion of it coincided with the laying of the foundations of his third building, the temple of Ares. This seems originally to have stood at Acharnai, but it was transported to Athens during the Augustan period and re-erected in the Athenian Agora, near the "Theseion." The final work produced by the architect of the temple at Sounion was the temple of Nemesis at Rhamnous (436 B.C.). Features common to all four of these buildings are the slender columns — compared with the Parthenon, with which they are contemporary —, the fact that the *antae* are aligned with the third column of the *pteron,* and a large number of Ionic influences, notably the relief frieze.

The metopes of the temple at Sounion had no relief decoration. All the relief sculptures were concentrated in a continuous frieze, placed inside the rectangular space between the colonnade of the façade and the line "connecting" the third column of each side with the *antae* and the two columns at the entrance to the *pronaos.* This feature was not repeated in the corresponding space behind the west façade of the building; this area marks yet another peculiar feature of the temple in that it is deeper than the area behind the eastern façade. The omission of the interior colonnade inside the *cella* was designed to leave more free space.

The cult statue of Poseidon, of which nothing is known, will have stood inside the *cella*. There was no means of communication between this and the *opisthodomos*, access to which could be gained only from the western entrance of the building. The *opisthodomos* will have housed the temple "treasury," and various precious dedications.

Three motifs have been detected in the relief scenes from the frieze: the Gigantomachy (Battle of the Gods and Giants), the Centauromachy (Battle of the Gods and Centaurs), and the Labours of Theseus. A number of slabs from the frieze can now be seen to the left of the *propylon*, before one climbs up to the temple. They are of Parian marble, and are in a very bad state of preservation; nonetheless, figures from the Gigantomachy can be recognised on some of them, as well as that of Artemis in her chariot, pulled by four horses. All that survives of the pedimental relief is the headless seated woman, now in the National Archaeological Museum, and the *anthemion* that stood as the *akroterion* above the centre of the pediment.

In addition to the sculptures, the temple was decorated with colourful paintings that will have given it an appearance very different from the gleaming white of today. It has been established that the paintings decorated the upper part of the capitals, the *sima* (gutter), the lower part of the horizontal *geison*, and other parts of the entablature. Fragments of the *geison* can be seen lying around the temple. Some pieces of the *sima* were found during the excavation of the Athenian Agora; they had been brought here during the Augustan period, along with the neighbouring temple of Athena, to be re-used in some unknown building.

The archaic *kouroi* and statue bases now in the National Archaeological Museum were discovered in front of the temple, only 3 m. from the bottom step of the entrance. A number of inscriptions were found in the sanctuary, one of which was of particular importance, since it referred to the sanctuary of Poseidon; it thus led to the proper identification of the building, which had previously been thought to be a temple of Athena. Shortly after the construction of the temple, Poseidon was dubbed *Souniaratos* by Aristophanes (*Birds* 559), but no weight had been attached to this testimony, and more tangible proof was needed before the temple could be identified.

From the stylobate of the temple there is a wonderful view of the neighbouring islands rising from the shimmering sea. On the one side lies Makronisos, with Kea beyond it, and on the other, to the right as one faces the tip of the promontory, is the island of Patroclos, with Aegina in the distance. One has the impression that one is looking down on them from a great height, though the stylobate is in fact no more than 73 m. above sea level. A total of 16 columns of the imposing temple of Poseidon are now standing, after a partial restoration, along with the two *antae* of the *pronaos*. Byron's name is carved on the *anta* to the right as

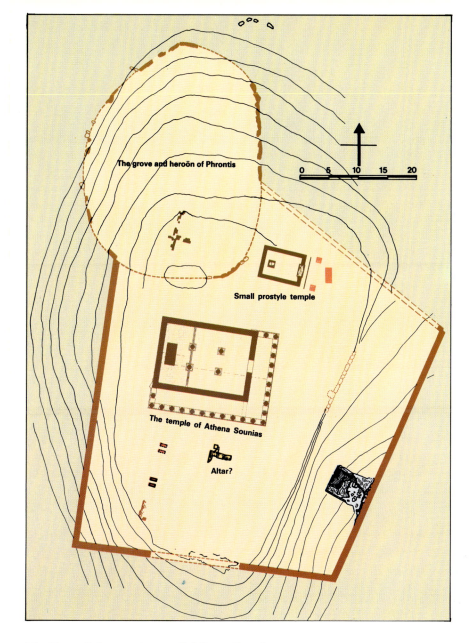

The grove and heroön of Phrontis

Small prostyle temple

The temple of Athena Sounias

Altar?

0 5 10 15 20

20. Plan of the sanctuary of Athena Sounias.

one enters the temple. Column drums and capitals were carried off to the West from time to time by the lovers of antiquity who visited the building. There is almost an entire column in Venice, and other pieces in England and Germany.

The fortress

The sanctuary of Poseidon covers only part of that area of the promontory that was walled on the landward side to form the fortress of Sounion. The sanctuary occupies the SE corner of the fortress, which had a total area of 9 acres. The excavator, V. Staïs came to the belief that the area was walled in the 6th century B.C. This interpretation has not found acceptance amongst recent scholars, however, who believe that the original wall was built in 421 B.C. during a critical phase of the Peloponnesian War. Important additions were made to the 5th century fortification during the course of the 3rd century B.C. The construction of these extensions was very costly, and the main part of them will have been built during the Macedonian occupation of Attica (263-229 B.C), though the Athenians will probably have been at pains to ensure that this important fortress was in good order, both during the Chremonidean War, which began in 267 B.C., and after the departure of the Macedonians.

The original wall, which was 3.50 m. wide and about 300 m. long, was strengthened by eleven square towers. The two sections of the wall enclosing the eastern and northern edges of the area are roughly the same length, and the angle between them was reinforced by a particularly powerful tower. The east section of the wall was stronger than that on the north, had more towers and was more carefully built. The northern section was more roughly constructed because the slope of the ground at this point offered a certain natural strength. The main entrance was at the west end of the northern section, at a point where the wall no longer survives. There was also a small, secondary gate in the E side, near the *peribolos* of the sanctuary. In the 5th century, a tower was built on the east side of the sanctuary wall in order to strengthen it at this point.

The original wall was polygonal, with large blocks of porous stone, but it has been faced in many places with isodomic masonry, also of porous stone, probably as a result of 3rd century improvements. The 3rd century also saw the construction of the striking bastion on the east side, which can be seen on the left just before the *propylon*. This bastion, which caused the small entrance on the eastern side to be abandoned, is a large building (area: 170 sq. m.) with careful isodomic masonry. The lower courses of the walls of it, which are preserved up to a height of 4 m., are made of marble, while the upper ones are of porous stone. The corners are rounded, to make it stronger, in conformity with the technique of the period.

Many different theories have been propounded as to the purpose of this building. An inscription discovered in this area led to its identification as a store for cereals, but since ammunition in the form of arrows and stone bullets was also found inside it, it is now thought that it was probably a general store for the supplies needed by the fortress, and it will also have served as a tower for defence purposes. Other interpretations that have been put forward include the view that it was used as an Athenian mint, or that it was the sanctuary of Phrontis, the hero buried at Sounion, according to Homer; as we shall see, however, his sanctuary was in the area of the sanctuary of Athena.

A new section of the defence wall was built in the 3rd century B.C. to reinforce part of the northern side near the sea, and to afford protection

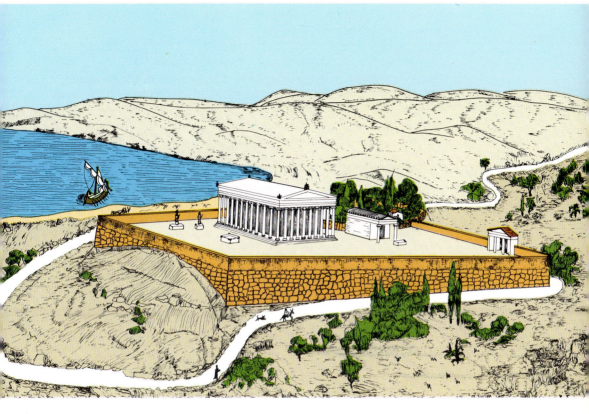

21. Reconstruction of the sanctuary of Athena Sounias.

for the two boathouses at the west end of this area. Both the wall and the building on the E side date from the period when Attica was captured by the forces of Antigonos Gonatas. This wall lay a short distance to the north of the first, with which it was almost parallel, and was reinforced by three towers.

The entrance to the fortress will have been a gate, that has not been preserved, between these two sections of the northern wall. It will have been totally inaccessible to the enemy, for his right side will have been exposed to fire from the towers on the later northern wall. The later section of the wall is faced with marble isodomic masonry.

The view from this point includes the walls and the boathouses below. These consist of two sloping ramps, 20.50 m. long and 11.50 m. wide, cut into the rock on the NW of the promontory, so that boats could be dragged up them. A staircase, of which only a few traces can be seen in the rock, led down to them from the fortress. The boathouses will have been protected by fortifications, but virtually nothing of these has survived. The harbour at Sounion lay to the west of them, at the site of the modern beach of Legrena. If one has the time to swim on this sandy beach one has a beautiful view of the promontory and can also easily gain access to the boathouses.

The entrance to the fortress was connected with the sanctuary by a road 4 m. wide. This has been excavated for a length of 90 m. and houses have been uncovered on both sides of it. The interior of the fortress has not been excavated systematically, but there appear to have been dwellings for the soldiers of the garrison and for the priests, and also houses belonging to the citizens of the ancient deme of Sounion. The area to the north of the ancient harbour was also occupied by *Sounieis*. A large house has been excavated near the northern section of the wall, which will have been associated with the defence of the 5th century entrance. The houses in the occupied area of the fortress included shrines that, according to the evidence of the inscriptions and reliefs, were dedicated to the cults of Asclepios, Aphrodite Pontia and Zeus Meilichios.

The sanctuary of Athena

The sanctuary of Athena is about 500 m. north-east of the fortress on a low hill, on the northern part of which there was a second sanctuary devoted to the cult of Phrontis. Very little has survived of these two sanctuaries, but it is worth visiting them for the marvellous view of the summit of the promontory and the temple of Poseidon.

The precinct of Athena, which has the shape of a trapezium, is bounded by a polygonal *peribolos*. Part of the northern section of this wall is hidden by the *peribolos* of the neighbouring sanctuary, which forms an irregular circle. This second, smaller precinct was a *heroön,* earlier in date than the sanctuary of Athena. It has been associated with Phrontis, Menelaos' helmsman, whose tomb was at Sounion, according to Homer.

The wall encircling the sanctuary of Athena encloses an area of 350 sq. m., within which can be seen the foundations of two buildings. The excavations here demonstrated that a number of *kouroi* stood in the sanctuary before the construction of the temple of Athena.

The great temple of Athena was known, before it was excavated, from the rather unclear description of it by the Roman architect Vitruvius (1st century B.C.), who includes it in his list of "abnormal" temples. The unusual feature of this Ionic temple was that the peristyle encloses only two sides of the *cella* — the east and south. It was built of marble from Agrileza, and its dimensions were approximately 19 m.×14.50 m. It had a total of 23 columns and gave the impression of a normal temple with 10×12 columns when viewed from the SE corner. The columns were very tall, and fluted; two of the fine capitals from this building are in the National Archaeological Museum, as we have already seen. The temple was removed to the Athenian Agora during the Augustan period, and a third capital is on display in the Agora Museum (in the Stoa of Attalos).

Inside the *cella,* which housed the statue of Athena, there were four

22. Reconstruction of the short side of the temple of Athena.

columns; two of them stood near the south wall of the *cella* and acted as supports for the roof, standing as they did on the central axis of the temple immediately below the ridge of the pedimental roof. The temple had no sculptures.

There is no general agreement as to its date: according to one view it was built in 470 B.C., a second would place it in the second half of the 5th century (possibly at the beginning of the Peloponnesian War), and a third distinguishes two building phases, the second of which saw the construction of the L-shaped peristyle, the columns in the *cella* and the new roof necessitated by the new shape of the building. A few blocks of porous stone survive from the foundations of an altar that stood in front of the south side of the temple.

The smaller temple is to the NE of the Ionic temple just described. The dimensions of this latter, 5×6.90 m., permitted only two Doric columns on the side where the entrance was; the square foundations of these columns are preserved. Inside the *cella* there is a base of grey Eleusinian stone that appears to have been used as a *kouros* base before it was moved to its present position. It is not absolutely certain that this small temple was dedicated to Athena. The theory has been advanced that it may have been dedicated to Artemis, the patron goddess of metal-workers; this would connect it with the mines nearby at Laurion. The temple was once thought to have been archaic (6th century B.C.), but it now seems to have been contemporary with, or even later than, the great temple of Athena. An altar was discovered in front of the entrance to it.

A number of interesting finds were made in the sanctuary of Athena, including the relief of the *Autostephanoumenos,* the small lead *kouros,* the head of a *kore,* and the fragments of *kouroi* mentioned above. Amongst the other discoveries (small Corinthian vases, clay busts, small tripods and bronze animals) there are some particularly fine painted Corinthian plates, one of which has a scene of hoplites being transported by ship.

23. The temple of Poseidon from the west.

24. *The temple of Poseidon and the propylaia of the sanctuary.*

25. *The propylaia of the sanctuary of Poseidon.*

26. *Remains of a tower and a gate in the fortification wall, with the west coast of Sounion in the background.*

25

26

27. *The temple of Poseidon from the south-east.*

28. *Part of a colonnade of the temple of Poseidon.*

29. *The inner part and colonnades of the temple of Poseidon.*

30. *The temple of Poseidon from the south.*

31. *The temple of Poseidon from the north.*

32. *Part of the north colonnade of the temple of Poseidon.*

33. *The temple of Poseidon from the south-east.*

34. *Part of the north colonnade of the temple of Poseidon.*

35. *The temple of Poseidon from the north-east.*

36. *The east side and entrance to the temple of Poseidon.*

37. *The temple of Poseidon from the east.*

38. *The temple of Poseidon from the north.*

37

38

39. *Part of the north anta of the temple of Poseidon showing the name of Lord Byron.*

40. *Part of the south colonnade of the temple of Poseidon.*

41. *Reliefs from the frieze of the temple of Poseidon.*

42. *The ruins of the temple of Athena Sounias, lying to the north-east of the temple of Poseidon.*

43. *The ruins of the smaller temple within the sanctuary of Athena Sounias.*

44. The ruins of the theatre at Thorikos, elliptic in shape and with stone seats.

45. The ruins at Thorikos. This settlement was already prosperous in prehistoric times and became a notable deme and an important stronghold of the Athenians in the classical period, but had declined by the 2nd century A.D.

46. View of the area around Thorikos.

FINDS FROM SOUNION
IN THE NATIONAL ARCHAEOLOGICAL MUSEUM
OF ATHENS

There are very few archaeological finds from Sounion dating from the prehistoric period; they become more numerous during the geometric period, and are plentiful from the 7th and 6th centuries onwards.

Most of the movable finds have been taken to the National Archaeological Museum in Athens, where some are on exhibition and others in storage. It is well worth seeing those that are on display, to complete the picture one forms of the two sanctuaries at Sounion.

A great change occurred in sculpture in the 7th and 6th centuries. The stone statues suddenly came alive and increased enormously in size. The predominant figure is that of the *kouros*: a naked youth with long hair, limbs arranged symmetrically, and the characteristic "archaic smile" on his lips.

A number of archaic *kouroi*, which had been erected in the sanctuary in the archaic period, were discovered in the fill that was deposited during the classical period in order to level off the area of the sanctuary of Poseidon. The two best preserved are on display in room 8 of the

47. Marble acroterion from the west pediment of the temple of Poseidon, consisting of two spirals surmounted by an anthemion, ca. 440 B.C.

Museum, along with the bases of two others. The best preserved of all (2720) is a colossal statue of a young man, with his left leg thrust forward and his shoulders sloping. It is a powerful, expressive piece of work from the end of the 7th century. The torso of the second *kouros* (3645) is from the same period (ca. 600 B.C.). It is thought to be by the same sculptor, though it is a maturer work and the plasticity of it is more advanced.

Room 14 contains objects from the early classical period, known to art historians as the period of the severe style (480-450 B.C.). Amongst them is a relief stele discovered in the sanctuary of Athena. It depicts a young man placing a crown on his head with his right hand, symbolising the honour he has been accorded for a victory in some athletic contest. The *Autostephanoumenos* (man crowning himself) is a very fine Attic work dating from the decade 470-460 B.C. The lower part of the stele is lost, and the legs of the figure are missing; the torso survives, however, along with the beautiful face, with its expression of complete inner calm. The young man will have offered this portrait of himself to the goddess on the occasion of his victory in the games. The stele is of Parian marble and the crown, the position of which is indicated by the series of holes by which it was attached, will probably have been made of some precious metal.

The finds from this same sanctuary dating from the archaic period — the head of a *kore,* and others — are not on display. Room 14, however, does contain two large Ionic capitals from the later temple of Athena (4478-4479). The more poorly preserved of the two contains traces of the painting with which the capitals of this temple were decorated. They are both fine examples of the art of their period (ca. 460 B.C.).

Very few architectural members from the temple of Poseidon were discovered during the excavations. A few fragments of the frieze are to be found in the area around the sanctuary, as we shall see during the description of the latter. Room 17 of the National Archaeological Museum contains a unique piece from the sculptures of the temple pediments: a headless, seated female figure. It is clear from its size (0.62 m. high) that this was one of the minor figures near the sharp angles of the pediments. It is thought to have been a nymph from the train of Poseidon. Like the temple itself, it is of local marble from Agrileza, and is dated, with reservations, to 430 B.C. The same room houses the *anthemion* that formed the central *akroterion* (ornamental finial of the pediment) of the temple; this is of Parian marble, as were other parts of the entablature.

48. Part of a relief stele found near the sanctuary of Athena Sounias. It depicts a youth placing a crown on his head with his right hand. He has a thin band around his head, and from the row of holes it appears that the crown was made of metal. The work is in Parian marble and is one of the finest pieces of Attic art, ca. 460 B.C.

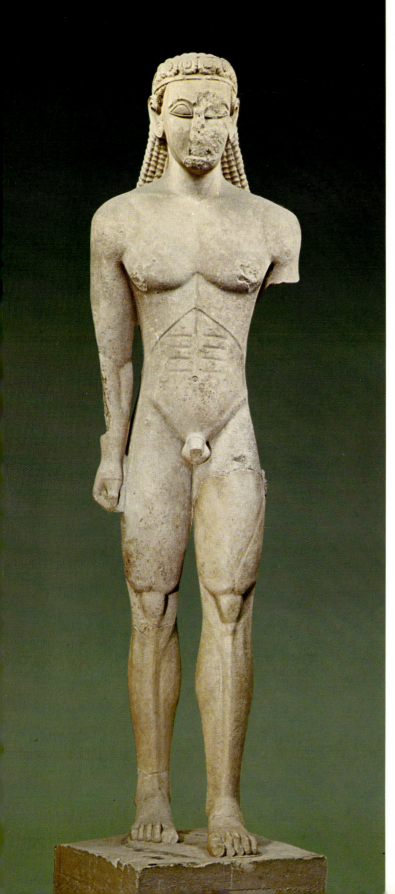

49. A colossal statue of a youth, a kouros, found at Sounion near the temple of Poseidon. The left leg is thrust forward and the arms held close to the sides. His long hair tied with a ribbon falls onto his back. An expressive and dynamic work dated from the end of the 7th century B.C.

50. Detail of the best-preserved archaic kouros from the sanctuary of Poseidon.

51. Small headless statue of a seated female figure, found at Sounion. It probably formed part of the pediment of the temple of Poseidon and perhaps depicts a nymph. It was carved in Agrileza marble, ca. 730 B.C.

52. The torso of a kouros, larger than life, found at Sounion together with the kouros of Fig. 49 and thought to be by the same sculptor. They are both dated ca. 600 B.C.

51

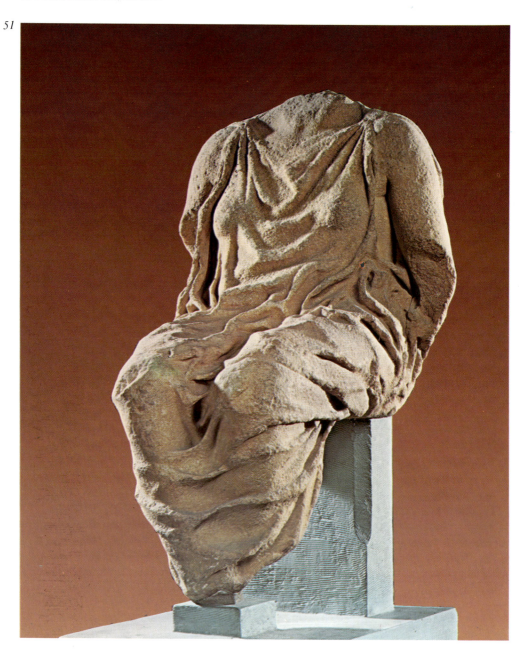

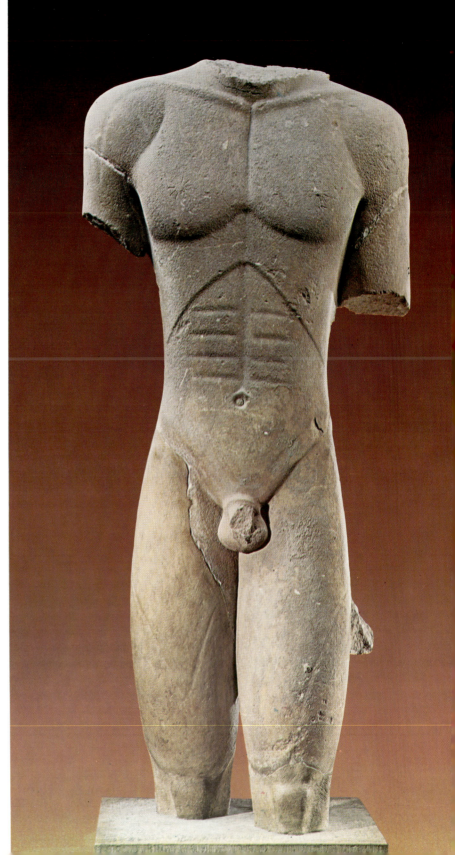

53

53. Plastic vase in the form of the head of a warrior wearing a helmet and cheekpieces to protect the vulnerable part of his head. The features are naturalistic and retain traces of colour. It was found in the sanctuary of Athena and is dated from the 6th century B.C.

54-55. Clay female busts from the archaic period. They are in the style of korai, differing only in points of detail such as the style of the hair and the facial features. They may depict goddesses. Found in the sanctuary of Athena Sounias, 6th century B.C.

54

55

56

57

56-57. *Corinthian ary-
balloi with represen-
tations of animals. They
have the usual painted
decoration and the
details are given by
means of short incised
lines. The background is
filled with a variety of
motifs, including rosettes
with radiating lines.
Found in the sanctuary
of Athena Sounias and
dated from the 7th-6th
centuries B.C.*

58. Painted clay Corinthian plaque depicting a warship transporting hoplites wearing helmets and carrying Boeotian shields and double spears. The oarsmen are not visible and are presumably hidden by the soldiers. From the sanctuary of Athena Sounias, 7th century B.C.

59. Bronze votive figurine from the sanctuary of Athena Sounias.

60. Lead kouros from the sanctuary of Athena Sounias. It is modelled on contemporary works of plastic art, except that the right leg is thrust forward instead of the left. The delicate workmanship in the facial features and in the formation of the body indicate that it copies an original and very advanced technique. 7th century B.C.

5

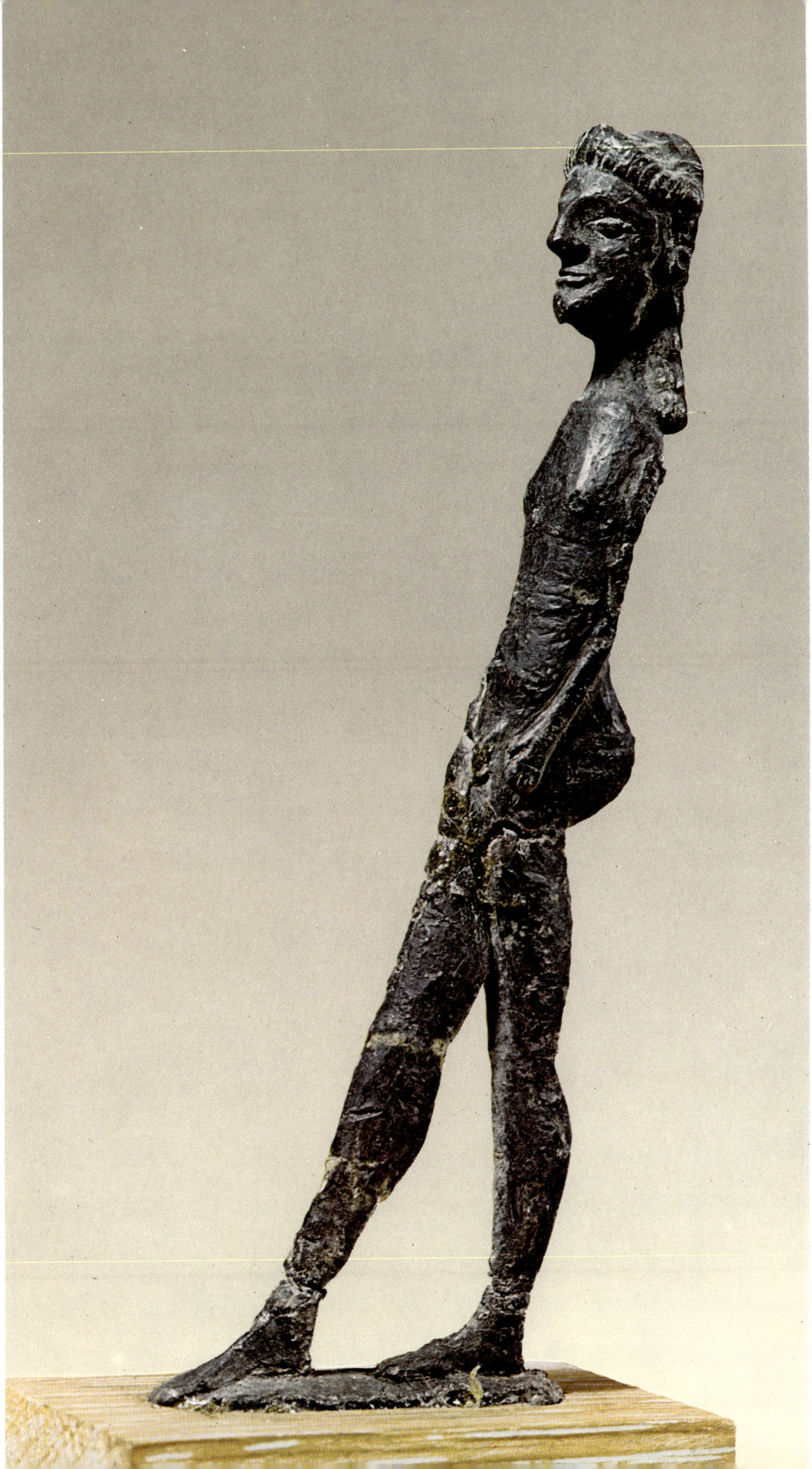

BIBLIOGRAPHY

BERVE, H.,-GRUBEN, G.,-HIRMER, M., *Greek temples, theatres and shrines.* London, 1963.

BESCHI, L., Disiecta membra del templo di Poseidon a capo Sunio. *Annuario, XLVII-XLVIII* (1969-70).

DELIVORRIAS, A., Poseidon-Tempel auf Kap Sunion. Neue Fragmente der Friesdekoration. *Athenische Mitteilungen*, 84 (1969).

DÖRIG, J., Sunionfriesplatte. *Athenische Mitteilungen*, 73 (1958).

DINSMOOR, W.B., The temple of Ares at Athens. *Hesperia*, IX (1940).

DINSMOOR, W.B. Jr., The temple of Poseidon. *American Journal of Archaeology*, 78 (1974).

HERBIG, R., Untersuchungen am dorischen peripteral Tempel auf Kap Sunion. *Athenische Mitteilungen*, 66 (1941).

ΚΑΡΟΥΖΟΥ, Σ., *Ἐθνικὸ Ἀρχαιολογικὸ Μουσεῖο. Συλλογή Γλυπτῶν.* Ἀθήνα, 1967.

KENNY, E.J.A., The ancient docks on the promontory of Sounion. *British School Annual*, XLII (1947).

MUSSCHE, H.F., Note sur les fortifications de Sounion. *Bulletin de Correspondance Hellénique*, XXXVIII (1964).

ΟΡΛΑΝΔΟΣ, A.K. Τὸ ἀέτωμα τοῦ ἐν Σουνίῳ ναοῦ τοῦ Ποσειδῶνος. *Ἀρχαιολογικὸν Δελτίον*, 1915.

— Ἡ γραπτὴ ἀρχιτεκτονικὴ διακόσμησις τοῦ ἐν Σουνίῳ ναοῦ τοῦ Ποσειδῶνος. *Ἀρχαιολογικὴ Ἐφημερίς*, 1953-54.

— Τοῦ ἐν Σουνίῳ ναοῦ τοῦ Ποσειδῶνος τοῖχος καὶ ὀροφή. *Ἀρχαιολογικὴ Ἐφημερίς*, 1917.

PLOMMER, W.H., Three attic temples. *British School Annual*, XLV (1950).

— The temple of Poseidon on Cape Sounion. Some further questions. *British School Annual*, 55 (1960).

PATON MORTON, J., *Chapters on Mediaeval and Renaissance visitors to Greek lands.* Princeton N.J., 1951.

ROBERTSON, D.S., *A handbook of Greek and Roman architecture.* Cambridge, 1946.

SCRANTON, R.L., *Greek Architecture.* London/New York, 1962.

— *Greek Walls.* Cambridge, 1941.

ΣΤΑΗΣ, Β., Ἀνασκαφαὶ ἐν Σουνίῳ. *Ἀρχαιολογικὴ Ἐφημερίς*, 1900, 1917.

— *Τὸ Σούνιον καὶ οἱ ναοὶ Ποσειδῶνος καὶ Ἀθηνᾶς.* Ἀθῆναι, 1920.

YOUNG, J.H., Studies in South Attica. Country estates at Sounion. *Hesperia*, XXV (1956).

The reconstructions of the temple of Poseidon (p. 35), the temple of Athena (p.41) and the sanctuary of Athena (p. 39) were carried out by the archaeologist Elsi Spathari. The reconstruction of the sanctuaries at Sounion published at the end of this volume is by the architect Elias Moutopoulos.

Maps and ground plans by Tonia Kotsoni.

SOUNION

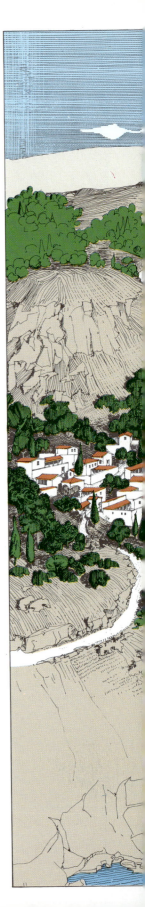

**Reconstruction of the sanctuaries
of Poseidon and Athena Sounias**

1. The temple of Sounion on the flat
summit of the headland.

2. The propylon.

3. The barracks for the garrison and
houses of civilians.

4. The boathouses in which the
warships were kept.

5. The entrance to the fortress.

6. A stoa and storehouses in the harbour.

7. The sanctuary of Athena Sounias.